COMIC-STRIP MATH

40 Reproducible Cartoons With Dozens of Funny Story Problems That Build Essential Math Skills

by Dan Greenberg

NIGHT SCHOOL featuring Woovis the Dog and Moovis the Cow

THE MOOVIS AND WOOVIS SHOW

I'm Moovis. He's Woovis.

Hey Moovis, I hear you're going to night school.

That's 100 percent correct.

Why night school?

I want to learn how to read in the dark.

Sigh.

YOU ANSWER IT!

1. In 1 hour, Moovis read 43 pages of a 212-page book called *The Big Moo*. Estimate how many hours it will take her to finish the book.

_____

SCHOLASTIC
PROFESSIONAL BOOKS

New York • Toronto • London • Auckland • Sydney

Cover and Interior design by Jaime Lucero for Grafica Inc.
Cover and interior illustrations by Jared Lee.

ISBN 0-590-18737-6

TABLE OF CONTENTS

TABLE OF CONTENTS

TOPICS CHART I

Use these charts to select reproducible pages that will fit the individual needs of each student in your class.

TITLE	PAGE	MAIN FOCUS	ADDITIONAL SKILLS
You Don't Say	9	Addition & Subtraction	Whole Numbers, Problem Solving
Late to Work	10	Addition & Subtraction	Time, Whole Numbers, Problem Solving
Round Trip	11	Addition & Subtraction	Map Reading, Whole Numbers, Estimation
The Texan	12	Addition & Subtraction	Map Reading, Whole Numbers, Estimation
Doggy Diner	13	Addition & Subtraction	Money, Decimals
Phoney Baloney	14	Place Value	Rounding, Decimals
Taxi, Taxi!	15	Reading a Schedule	Time, Computation
Rabbit Feet	16	Multiplication & Division	Whole Numbers, Problem Solving
Seven Ker-plunk!	17	Mutliplication & Division	Whole Numbers, Problem Solving
Stairway to the Top	18	Multiplication & Division	Whole Numbers, Problem Solving
Go Skating	19	Multiplication & Division	Whole Numbers, Money, Problem Solving
Mouse Trap	20	Multiplication & Division	Whole Numbers, Money, Problem Solving
Camouflage	21	Division & Multiplication	Whole Numbers, Problem Solving
Non-Toxic	22	Division & Multiplication	Time, Whole Numbers, Problem Solving
Carrot Soup	23	Division & Multiplication	Patterns, Problem Solving, Whole Numbers
Golf Pro	24	Division & Multiplication	Money, Decimals, Problem Solving
Night School	25	Estimation	Money, Division & Multiplication
The Big Deal	26	Estimation	Money, Addition & Subtraction
The Day of the Dentist	27	Word Problems	Problem Solving, Whole Numbers
Politics	28	Word Problems	Problem Solving, Whole Numbers

TOPICS CHART II

TITLE	PAGE	MAIN FOCUS	ADDITIONAL SKILLS
Baseball Fever	29	Fractions	Lowest Terms, Comparing Fractions
Doctor Knows Best	30	Fractions	Addition & Subtraction, Measurement
New Boots	31	Fractions	Addition & Subtraction, Mixed Numbers
Stubbed	32	Fractions	Addition & Subtracton, Mixed Numbers
Dance Fever	33	Fractions	Multiplication, Problem Solving
What's Hoppin'?	34	Fractions	Multiplication, Comparing, Problem Solving
Burnt Cake	35	Fractions	Time, Mixed Numbers, Multiplication
Leftovers	36	Fractions	Multiplication & Division, Problem Solving
Doctor Knows Best Again	37	Bar Graph	Multiplication & Division, Statistics
What's Hoppin' Again?	38	Plotting	Problem Solving, Working with Direction
New Job	39	Pictograph	Drawing a Graph, Time, Addition & Subtraction
Special Delivery	40	Measurement	Unit Conversion, Multiplication
Money Back	41	Geometry	Square Units, Multiplication, Area, Perimeter
Fun Box	42	Geometry	Perimeter, Decimals, Multiplication
Pie & Pi	43	Geometry	Circumference, Diameter, Radius, Decimals
Snoozer	44	Rate	Multiplication & Division, Time, Decimals
Pulsations	45	Rate	Large Numbers, Multiplication & Division, Time
Hums	46	Rate	Large Numbers, Multiplication & Division, Time
Speed Trap	47	Rate	Miles Per Hour, Time, Multiplication & Division
Family Reunion Picnic	48	Ratio	Percent, Lowest Terms, Decimals, Computation

ABOUT THIS BOOK

The purpose of this book should be clear from its title: to make math fun! The cartoons on these pages are fun. But they also have a serious job—to give students context. Math, after all, is ultimately about solving problems in a particular situation. The more interesting the situation, the more motivated most students are to pursue mathematical goals. This book provides contexts—40 of them—that students can really sink their teeth into.

Using funny characters and a whimsical point of view, the cartoons on these pages explore a variety of critical mathematical topics that are specified by the National Council of Teachers of Mathematics Curriculum Standards. Topics focus on basic number operations—addition, subtraction, multiplication, and division—and cover such elements as fractions, decimals, estimation, mental math, measurement, geometry, and graphing.

Additional topics include ratio and percent, rounding, writing and solving equations, formulas, mapping, time, and money math. The book also contains plenty of problem-solving activities that encourage students to use such problem-solving skills as guess and check, work backwards, make a table, and draw a diagram.

USING THIS BOOK

The book is divided into 7 sections: Addition, Subtraction, and Place Value; Multiplication and Division; Estimation and Word Problems; Fractions; Graph Reading; Measurement and Geometry; and Rate, Ratio, and Percent.

Check the Main Focus that appears in the Table of Contents and at the top of each page. The Topics Chart gives an in-depth analysis of the skills covered on each page. Within each section, topics get progressively more challenging. Thus, the beginning cartoons in a section may focus on basic facts while the later topics apply knowledge in increasingly sophisticated ways.

The final "Wrap It Up" problem on each page functions as an extension, encouraging students to draw pictures or diagrams, make models, collect data, and create their own problems.

Complete answers are on pages 49–55.

In the classroom, the cartoons can be employed in a variety of ways including:
• Whole class participation: Students work together to solve problems.
• Small group participation: This allows teams of students to find solutions on their own.
• Individual participation either as work in class, homework, or self-paced study.

REMEMBER TO HAVE FUN!

My hope for this book is to not only amuse and educate, but to also open students' eyes about math's possibilities. If math is fun on these pages, it can be fun anywhere. Once students realize this, there is no telling what they will accomplish!

Name: _____

YOU DON'T SAY featuring Woovis the Dog and Moovis the Cow

YOU ANSWER IT!

1. In their comedy act, Moovis and Woovis told 7 utterly funny jokes and 4 udderly funny jokes. How many jokes did they tell in all?

_____

2. Woovis told 16 dog biscuit jokes. The audience laughed at all but 7 of them. How many dog biscuit jokes did the audience laugh at? _____

3. Nine of Moovis's 14 cow jokes were "udderly" ridiculous. How many jokes were not udderly ridiculous? _____

4. Woovis and Moovis were on stage for a total of 45 minutes. Before the intermission, they were on stage for 21 minutes. How long were they on stage after the intermission? _____

5. After intermission, Woovis told 3 fewer jokes than Moovis. Moovis told 11 cow jokes. How many jokes did Woovis tell after intermission? _____

6. The Woovis and Moovis Show played for 5 nights in New York. The show played for twice as many nights in Chicago than it played in New York. How many nights did the show play in all? _____

7. In New York, Woovis and Moovis were paid a combined total of $10 for each show. But Woovis earned $2 more for each show than Moovis earned. How much did each animal earn for each show? _____

WRAP IT UP! The Woovis and Moovis Show needs jokes. Can you help them out? Find or make up a good joke that has a math problem in it. Then write your joke and display it in class. Add pictures if you wish!

9

Name: _____

LATE TO WORK featuring Judy Frog and Sal and Al Gator

YOU ANSWER IT!

1. Judy slept from 10 p.m. Saturday to 8 a.m. Sunday. How many hours did she sleep in all? _____

2. Judy normally goes to bed at 9 p.m. and wakes up at 6:30 a.m. How many hours of sleep is that? _____

3. One night Judy stays up late and goes to bed at 10:30 p.m. What time should she wake up the next day to get her normal amount of sleep? _____

4. Al Gator normally goes to bed at 9:30 p.m. and gets up at 8:30 a.m. On Wednesday, Al went to bed an hour later and got up an hour earlier Thursday morning. How many hours did he sleep? _____

5. On Thursday, Al went to sleep an hour and a half earlier than normal. He got up an hour and a half earlier than his normal wake-up time. How many hours did he sleep? _____

6. Judy worked for 5 hours. She worked from 9:30 a.m. to 11 a.m. Then she took a break for 1 hour. How long did she work after her break? _____

7. Al worked for 4 hours. Each hour he took a 15-minute break. How many hours did he actually work? _____

8. Judy's clock runs an hour fast. Suppose her clock says the time is 8:30 p.m. when she goes to sleep. What is the actual time? _____

WRAP IT UP! Judy needs 2 hours to get ready for work. If her clock is 1 hour fast, for what time should she set her alarm to arrive at work at an actual time of 8:30 a.m.?

_____

Name: _____

ROUND TRIP featuring Woovis the Dog and Harry the Horse

YOU ANSWER IT!

1. How far is a trip from the Old Travel Agency to the Old Mill and back? _____
_____

2. How long is a trip from the Old Travel Agency to the Old Tree, to the Old Barn, and back to the Old Travel Agency?

_____

3. How long is a trip from the Old Travel Agency, to the Old Tree, to the Old Barn, back to the Old Tree, to the Old Mill, back to the Old Tree, then back to the Old Travel Agency? _____

_____

4. What is the shortest trip that begins at the Old Travel Agency and ends at the Old Pond? _____

_____

5. Woovis went from the Old Travel Agency to the Old Tree. Then he went to one other place before coming back to the Old Travel Agency. He went 13 miles in all. Where did Woovis go? _____

_____

6. Which route from the Old Travel Agency to the Old Pond covers 9 miles? _____

_____

_____

7. Which route from the Old Travel Agency to the Old Pond covers 17 miles? _____

_____

_____

WRAP IT UP! Use Harry's travel map to make up some story problems for a friend to try.

Name: _____

THE TEXAN featuring Rowena Pig and Squirmy Worm

Speech bubbles:
- I was born in Texas.
- What part?
- Why all of me, of course.
- Har dee har.

Map labels:
- Lubbock
- 345
- 319
- Ft. Worth
- Dallas
- El Paso
- 589
- 28
- 642
- Austin
- 192
- 245
- 564
- 78
- 197
- Houston
- San Antonio
- 354
- 274
- Brownsville

YOU ANSWER IT!

1. Squirmy wants to travel from El Paso to Lubbock. How many miles are between the 2 cities. Use the map below to answer the question.

_____

2. After going from El Paso to Lubbock, Squirmy went to Forth Worth. How many miles did he travel in all? _____

3. Rowena traveled straight from El Paso to Forth Worth. How many fewer miles did Rowena travel than Squirmy? _____

4. How many miles would a round-trip between Houston and Brownsville cover? _____

5. Which route from Dallas to Brownsville covers 544 miles? _____

6. Which route from San Antonio to Lubbock covers 789 miles? _____

_____

7. Which is the shortest route from San Antonio to Lubbock? _____

_____

WRAP IT UP! Find a route that goes through every city on the map. Write it down on a separate sheet of paper. How many miles is your route?

DOGGY DINER featuring Woovis the Dog and Rowena Pig

Hmm . . .

Woovis Diner

Waiter, is there any gravy on the menu?

Menu

There was, but I wiped it all off with a napkin.

YOU ANSWER IT!

1. How much would 2 Trough Dinners cost?

_____

TROUGH MENU

TROUGH DINNER -- $4.95
MUSH (CUP) ------ $1.99
    (BOWL) ---- $2.49
SCRAPS ---------- $1.25
SWILL ------------ $1.50
REGULAR SLOP---- $3.95
DELUXE SLOP------ $4.95

2. How much would a Trough Dinner and an order of Regular Slop cost?

_____

3. How much will a cup of Mush, one order of Scraps, and one order of Swill cost? _____

4. Rowena has $15. Is that enough money to buy 3 Trough Dinners? Why or why not?_____

_____

5. Can Rowena buy a cup of Mush and one order of Scraps with $5? If so, how much change will she get back?

_____

6. Which costs more, 5 orders of Regular Slop or 4 orders of Deluxe Slop?

_____

7. Rowena ordered Regular Slop, a bowl of Mush, and one other item. She spent a total of $7.69. What other item did she order? _____

8. Rowena's friend Purvis has $10 and wants 2 orders of Regular Slop and 1 Trough Dinner. How much more money does he need? _____

9. How much money would Rowena need to buy 2 of everything on the menu?

_____

WRAP IT UP! Make a coupon for a special discount on an item at the Woovis Diner. Show how it would change your answer to one of the problems above.

Name: _____

PHONEY BALONEY featuring Steve Hummingbird and Ant Betty

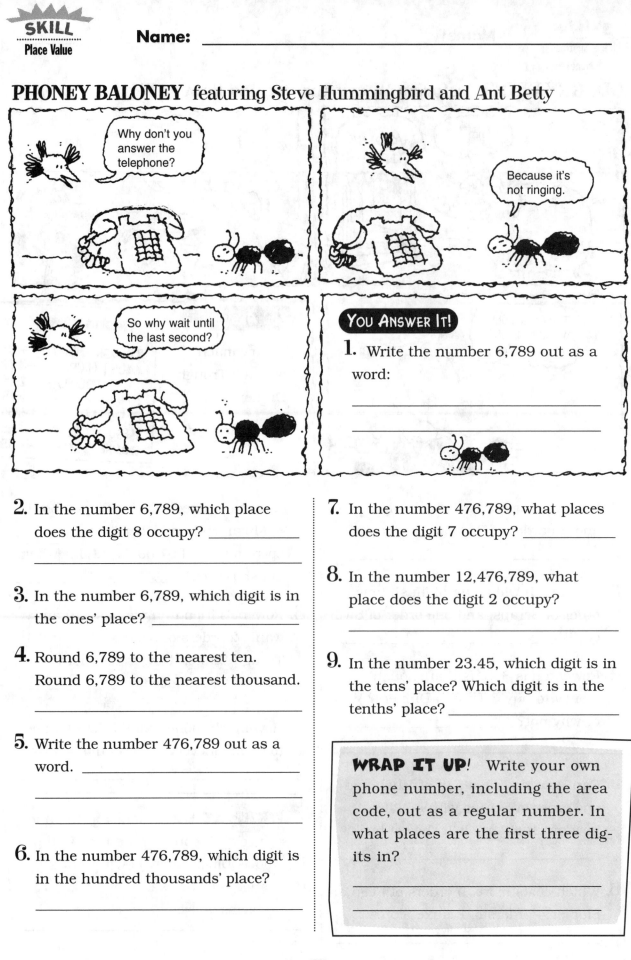

Why don't you answer the telephone?

Because it's not ringing.

So why wait until the last second?

YOU ANSWER IT!

1. Write the number 6,789 out as a word:

   _____

   _____

2. In the number 6,789, which place does the digit 8 occupy? _____
   _____

3. In the number 6,789, which digit is in the ones' place? _____

4. Round 6,789 to the nearest ten. Round 6,789 to the nearest thousand.
   _____

5. Write the number 476,789 out as a word. _____
   _____
   _____

6. In the number 476,789, which digit is in the hundred thousands' place?
   _____

7. In the number 476,789, what places does the digit 7 occupy? _____

8. In the number 12,476,789, what place does the digit 2 occupy?
   _____

9. In the number 23.45, which digit is in the tens' place? Which digit is in the tenths' place? _____

WRAP IT UP! Write your own phone number, including the area code, out as a regular number. In what places are the first three digits in?

_____

_____

Name: _____

TAXI, TAXI! featuring Rowena Pig and Squirmy Worm

YOU ANSWER IT!

1. The movie *Pigs Have More Fun* starts at 11:15 and lasts 1 hour and 30 minutes. What time will the movie end? _____

2. The theater showing *Pigs Have More Fun* runs the movie throughout the day. Each show starts 15 minutes after the previous one ends. If the first show starts at 11:15 a.m., what time does the second one begin? _____
_____

3. What time does the third showing start? If Woovis arrives at 3 p.m. will he be in time to see the beginning of the movie? _____
_____

4. Harry the Horse wants to see the movie after 6 p.m. But he needs to be home by 8:30 p.m. Can he see the movie? _____
_____

5. Between 11:15 a.m. and 9:45 p.m., how many times is *Pigs Have More Fun* shown at the beginning of an hour? _____

6. This theater also shows the movie *Citizen Pig* every 2 hours and 15 minutes. starting at 11:30 a.m. What time will *Citizen Pig* be shown between 3 p.m. and 5 p.m.? _____

7. Is there a time when *Citizen Pig* and *Pigs Have More Fun* are showing at the same time? _____

WRAP IT UP! Make up your own fake movie schedule. Then write some problems for a friend to try.

Name: _____

RABBIT FEET featuring Woovis the Dog and Rudy the Red-Nosed Rabbit

Hey Woovis, when do rabbits have 20 feet?

I don't know, Rudy. When?

When there are 5 rabbits. Get it?

YOU ANSWER IT!

1. A rabbit has 4 feet. How many feet do 4 rabbits have? _____

2. A group of rabbits has a total of 24 feet. How many rabbits are in the group? _____

3. A starfish has 5 legs. Four starfish were doing underwater cartwheels. How many legs were doing cartwheels? _____

4. A beetle has 6 legs. A total of 22 beetles bought basketball sneakers. How many sneakers did they buy?

_____

5. Basketball sneakers come in pairs of 2. How many *pairs* of basketball sneakers did the beetles buy?

_____

6. A group of eight-legged spiders with a total of 48 legs is walking with a group of rabbits that have a total of 12 legs. How many animals are walking? _____

_____

7. Two spiders and 1 rabbit leave the walking group. Five people join the group. How many legs are walking in all? _____

8. There are 5 people, 2 rabbits, 22 beetles, and 4 spiders. How many legs are there in all? _____

WRAP IT UP! Draw a cartoon that shows your how you solved one of the problems on this page.

Name: _____

SEVEN-KERPLUNK! featuring Woovis the Dog and Wendy Spider

What goes 7-kerplunk!, 7-kerplunk!, 7-kerplunk! in the middle of the night?

I have no idea.

A spider with a broken leg out for a moonlight stroll.

YOU ANSWER IT!

1. Sam Spider takes 5 steps with each of his 8 legs. How many steps does he take in all?

_____

2. Sharon Spider takes 72 steps in all. How many steps does she take with each of her 8 legs? _____

3. Susan Spider takes 14 steps with each of her 8 legs. How many more steps does she take than Sharon in problem 2? _____

4. Mike Spider takes 7 rounds of steps. Then he takes 23 rounds of steps. How many steps did he take in all?

_____

5. Wendy Spider has a cast on her broken leg. She takes 7 steps with with her broken leg. In total, how many steps does she take with her other 7 legs?

_____

6. Wendy stops for a rest. Then she takes 10 steps with each of her 8 legs. Including the steps she took in problem 5, how many steps did she take in all? _____

7. How many more steps did Wendy take with her broken leg after resting (problem 5) than she took with her broken leg before resting (problem 6)?

_____

8. Gary Grasshopper takes 26 steps with each of his 6 legs. Does he take more steps than the total number of steps taken by all the spiders in problems 1, 2, 3? _____

WRAP IT UP! Make up a problem about a centipede with 1 or more broken legs. Trade problems with a friend and solve each other's problem.

Name: _____

STAIRWAY TO THE TOP featuring Squirmy Worm and Ant Betty

Hey Squirmy, will these stairs take me to the 5th floor?

No, Ant Betty. You need to walk to get to the 5th floor.

Ha ha. That's so funny I forgot to laugh.

YOU ANSWER IT!

1. Each staircase had 9 steps. How many staircases did Ant Betty climb to get from the 1st floor to the 3rd floor? How many steps did she climb? _____

2. Ant Betty went from the 3rd floor to the 8th floor. How many steps did she climb? _____

3. Squirmy started on the 2nd floor and walked up 27 steps. What floor did he end up on? _____

4. Squirmy walked from the basement to the 6th floor. How many steps did he walk up? _____

5. Squirmy walked from the 8th floor to the basement. How many steps did he descend? _____

6. Ant Betty started on the 2nd floor and walked up 45 steps. Then she walked down 18 steps. On which floor did she end up? _____

7. Ant Betty walked up 36 steps from the 1st floor. Squirmy walked down 27 steps from the 8th floor. On which floor did each of them end up?

_____

_____

8. Ant Betty went to another building that has 12 steps in each staircase. How many steps did she need to climb to go from floor 1 to floor 4?

_____

WRAP IT UP! Suppose the first building had 7-step staircases on each floor instead of 9. How would that change your answer to problem 2?

_____

GO SKATING featuring Woovis, Harry the Horse, and Judy the Frog

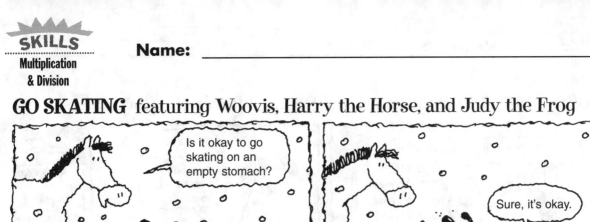

YOU ANSWER IT!

1. It costs 35 cents to rent 1 pair of skates. Woovis has 4 legs and needs 2 pairs of skates. How much will it cost him to rent 2 pairs of skates? _____

2. It costs $2.75 to skate at the rink. Woovis rents 2 pairs of skates. How much will it cost him to rent skates and skate at the rink? _____

3. Woovis and Judy each rent 2 pairs of skates. What will be the total cost for both of them to rent skates and skate at the rink? _____

4. Wendy Spider has 8 legs. She needs 4 pairs of skates. How much will it cost her to rent skates and skate at the rink? _____

5. Tiger Jones and Fangella the Snake went skating. Tiger owns his own skates. Fangella rents 1 pair of skates. How much will it cost the two of them to go skating? _____

6. Squirmy Worm has 12 legs. Rudy the Red-Nosed Rabbit has 4 legs. How much will it cost the two of them to rent skates and go skating? _____

7. Harry and his 3 cousins went to the rink. Harry and one of the cousins brought their own skates. How much did all 4 spend to skate? _____

8. An animal with no skates pays $3.80 to rent skates and skate at the rink. How many legs does the animal have?

_____

WRAP IT UP! How much would it cost a family of 16 rabbits to skate with rented skates? How much would they save if they brought their own skates?

_____

_____

19

Name: _____

MOUSE TRAP featuring Woovis the Dog and Harry the Horse

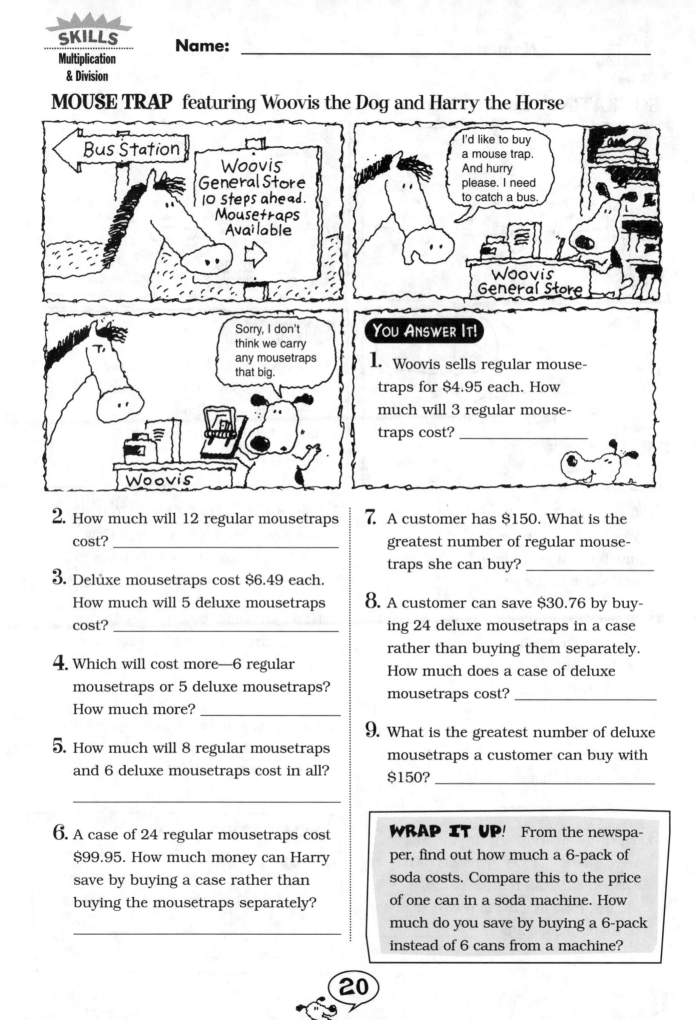

2. How much will 12 regular mousetraps cost? _____

3. Deluxe mousetraps cost $6.49 each. How much will 5 deluxe mousetraps cost? _____

4. Which will cost more—6 regular mousetraps or 5 deluxe mousetraps? How much more? _____

5. How much will 8 regular mousetraps and 6 deluxe mousetraps cost in all?

_____

6. A case of 24 regular mousetraps cost $99.95. How much money can Harry save by buying a case rather than buying the mousetraps separately?

_____

7. A customer has $150. What is the greatest number of regular mousetraps she can buy? _____

8. A customer can save $30.76 by buying 24 deluxe mousetraps in a case rather than buying them separately. How much does a case of deluxe mousetraps cost? _____

9. What is the greatest number of deluxe mousetraps a customer can buy with $150? _____

WRAP IT UP! From the newspaper, find out how much a 6-pack of soda costs. Compare this to the price of one can in a soda machine. How much do you save by buying a 6-pack instead of 6 cans from a machine?

Name: _____

CAMOUFLAGE featuring Woovis the Dog and Moovis the Cow

THE MOOVIS AND WOOVIS SHOW

I'm Woovis. She's Moovis.

Hey, did you know cows sometimes paint themselves yellow and gold in the fall.

No I didn't. Why do they do that?

So they can hide in maple treetops and blend in with the fall colors.

Really? I've never seen a cow hiding in a tree before.

See how well it works!

YOU ANSWER IT!

1. A total of 32 cows hid in the tops of 4 maple trees. Each tree held the same number of cows. How many cows were in each tree? _____

2. A tree held 24 birds and 8 cows. How many animals were in the tree? _____

3. Forty-eight cows hid in the tops of some trees. Each tree held 8 cows. How many trees were there in all?

_____

4. There were 5 trees in a yard. If 7 cows hid in each tree, how many cows were there in all? _____

5. A total of 54 cows found 9 trees to hide in. The same number of cows hid in each tree. How many cows hid in each tree? _____

6. A cow gave 6 buckets of milk each day for 12 days. How many buckets did it give in all? _____

7. Woovis and Moovis were on the road for 56 days. How many 7-day weeks did they spend on the road? _____

8. A sheep dog herded 84 cows into 4 equal-sized groups. How many cows were in each group? _____

9. Going to sleep, Woovis counted 96 cows jumping over a fence in 6 minutes. If he counted an equal number of cows each minute, how many cows jumped the fence each minute? _____

WRAP IT UP! Draw a cartoon problem of colorful cows hiding in trees. Make sure your problem asks a math question. Then display your cartoon for classmates to solve.

Name: _____

NON-TOXIC featuring Squirmy Worm and Fangella the Snake

Boy am I glad I'm not a poisonous snake.

How come?

I just bit my tongue.

Yikes!

YOU ANSWER IT!

1. Fangella sticks out her tongue once every 4 seconds. There are 60 seconds in 1 minute. How many times will she stick it out in 1 minute? _____

2. How many times will Fangella stick out her tongue in 3 minutes? _____

3. How many times will Fangella stick her tongue out in a half an hour (or 30 minutes)? _____

4. Fangella is 48 inches long. Squirmy is 4 inches long. How many times longer is Fangella than Squirmy?

_____

5. Fangella traveled 60 miles to the Snake Convention. It took her 4 days to get there and she traveled the same number of miles each day. How many miles did she travel each day? _____

6. There were 258 snakes at the Snake Convention. They split up into 6 equal-sized groups. How many snakes were in each group? _____

7. Fangella belonged to the Mini-Viper snake group. She collected $12 from all 43 members of the group for T-shirts. How much did Fangella collect?

_____

8. The Mega-Viper snake group collected $378 for its T-shirts. If each shirt cost only $9, how many snakes were in the group? _____

WRAP IT UP! Make a design for a snake T-shirt. Write a division fact such as 24 ÷ 8 = 3 on your shirt design. Display your designs in class.

Name: _____

CARROT SOUP featuring Squirmy Worm and Rudy the Red-Nosed Rabbit

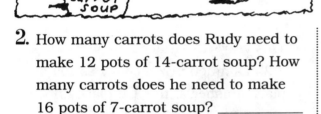

YOU ANSWER IT!

1. Rudy has 58 carrots. How many pots of 14-carrot soup could he make? How many leftover carrots would he have?

_____

2. How many carrots does Rudy need to make 12 pots of 14-carrot soup? How many carrots does he need to make 16 pots of 7-carrot soup? _____

_____

3. How many pots of 14-carrot soup can Rudy make with 126 carrots? How many pots of 7-carrot soup can Rudy make with the same number of carrots?

_____

4. How many pots of 7-carrot soup can Rudy make with 100 carrots? How many carrots will be left over? _____

_____

5. Rudy has 63 carrots. How many pots of 7-carrot soup can he make? How many pots of 14-carrot soup? How many carrots will be left over? _____

6. Rudy made 10 pots of 7-carrot soup and had 3 carrots left over. How many carrots did he have when he started?

_____

7. Rudy made 10 pots of 14-carrot soup. How many pots of 7-carrot soup can he make with the same number of carrots?

_____

8. Rudy made 100 pots of 14-carrot soup. How many pots of 7-carrot soup can he make with the same number of carrots? _____

WRAP IT UP! Make a table that shows how many pots of 7-carrot soup and 14-carrot soup you can make with 42 carrots, 56 carrots, 70 carrots, and 84 carrots. What pattern do you see? How could you use the pattern to solve other soup problems?

Name: _____

GOLF PRO featuring Woovis the Dog and Tiger Jones

Hey Woovis, why should you wear 2 hats when you're playing golf?

I don't know. Why?

In case you get a hole in one.

YOU ANSWER IT!

1. The Tiger Jones Golf Tournament features $100,000 in prize money. If 8 players split the prize money equally, how much will each player win?_____

2. How much in prize money will each player win if they split $100,000 equally among 16 players? _____

3. How many players would there be if they split up the $100,000 equally and each player got $5,000? _____

4. Last year the $100,000 prize money was split among the top 3 players only. The winner got half of the money, and the remaining 2 players split up the rest equally. How much did each player get?

_____

_____

5. This year the winner won 2.6 as much prize money as the 2nd place finisher. If the 2nd place finisher won $20,000, how much did the winner win?

_____

6. This year's 3rd place finisher won 2.25 as much prize money as the 4th place finisher. If the 3rd place finisher got $9,000, how much did the 4th place finisher win? _____

7. The 5th and 6th place finishers won 0.75 as much as the 4th place finisher above. How much did they each win? _____

WRAP IT UP! Create a prize money scheme in which the winner gets twice as much as the 2nd place finisher. The 2nd place finisher gets twice as much as the 3rd place finisher. The 3rd place finisher gets twice as much as the 4th place finisher, and so on. How much does each player win?

Name: _____

NIGHT SCHOOL featuring Woovis the Dog and Moovis the Cow

THE MOOVIS AND WOOVIS SHOW

I'm Moovis. He's Woovis.

Hey Moovis, I hear you're going to night school.

That's 100 percent correct.

Why night school?

I want to learn how to read in the dark.

Sigh.

YOU ANSWER IT!

1. In 1 hour, Moovis read 43 pages of a 212-page book called *The Big Moo*. Estimate how many total hours it will take her to finish the book. _____

2. Woovis read 29 pages of *The Big Moo* in 1 hour. Remember, the book has 212 pages. About how many total hours will it take him to finish the book? _____

3. Woovis can read *Moo Over Miami* twice as fast as he can read *The Big Moo*. About how many pages of *Moo Over Miami* can he read in 6 hours? _____

4. *Moo over Miami* has 532 pages. About how many hours will it take Woovis to read the entire book if he reads at the same rate he read in problem 3?

_____

5. Moovis read 48 pages of *Moo Over Miami* in one hour. About how many hours will it take her to read the entire 532-page book? _____

6. Moovis wants to buy 2 books. Which books can she buy for under $5? For under $6? For under $10?

The Moo Lagoon $5.95

COW FOR A DAY $3.75

THE BIG MOO $2.50

Moo Over Miami $1.95

_____
_____
_____
_____

7. To the nearest dollar, how much money does Woovis need to buy all 4 books? _____

WRAP IT UP! Find the price of *Comic-Strip Math* (or any other book). How many $10-bills would you need to buy 3 copies of this book? Explain.

Name: _____

THE BIG DEAL featuring Woovis the Dog and Wendy Spider

2. Wendy bought a notebook that costs $3.15 and stickers that cost $1.79. Is the total cost closer to $3.00, $5.00, or $10.00? _____

3. Woovis went to the movies. A movie ticket cost $5.75. What was the cost of 1 movie ticket rounded to the nearest dollar? _____

4. Woovis paid for his ticket with $10.00. How much change did he get back rounded to the nearest dollar? _____

5. Woovis bought popcorn. The popcorn cost $3.19. What was the cost of the popcorn rounded to the nearest dollar?

_____

6. What was the cost of Woovis's popcorn rounded to the nearest 10 cents?

7. Woovis also bought a soda for $2.85. What was the total amount of money he spent at the movies rounded to the nearest dollar? _____

8. Wendy bought a pair of jeans for $36.99, a hat for $8.65, and a coat for $52.49. What was the total cost of all 3 items rounded to the nearest dollar?

_____

9. Wendy paid for the items with $100.00. With the change she got back, could she have bought 3 packs of gum that cost a total of $1.90? _____

WRAP IT UP! Find a newspaper ad that includes prices for something you want. Make up a problem requiring estimation using the prices in the ad.

Name: _____

THE DAY OF THE DENTIST featuring Tiger Jones and Wendy Spider

Panel 1: Yow! The dentist fixed my sore tooth.

Panel 2: Does your tooth still hurt?

Panel 3: I don't know. The dentist kept the tooth after she pulled it out.

Duh.

YOU ANSWER IT!

1. Tiger had 7 teeth when he was a baby. Now he has 3 times as many teeth. How many teeth does Tiger have now? _____

2. Tiger Jones has 11 more stripes than Tiger Smith. Tiger Jones has 46 stripes. How many stripes does Tiger Smith have? _____

3. Tiger Brown has 14 fewer stripes than Tiger Jones. Does Tiger Brown have fewer stripes than Tiger Smith? _____
_____

4. Tiger's dentist saw twice as many patients today as she saw yesterday. She saw 12 patients today. How many did she see yesterday? _____

5. A spider has 8 legs. A group of spiders has a total of 32 legs. How many spiders are there in the group?
_____

6. Seven tigers are standing near the group of spiders from question 5. If each tiger has 4 legs, which group has more total legs, the tigers or the spiders? _____

7. One spider leaves the spider group from problem 6. Three tigers join the tiger group. How many animal legs are there in all? _____
_____

WRAP IT UP! Tiger Jones played for 8 hours on Saturday. That is twice as long as he played on Friday and half as long as he played on Sunday. How much longer did he play on Sunday than he played on Friday? _____
_____
_____

Name: _____

POLITICS featuring Woovis the Dog and Fangella the Snake

Who lives in the White House, is elected every 4 years, and speaks with a forked tongue?

I don't know. Who?

The President of the United Snakes.

YOU ANSWER IT!

1. One term for the President of the United Snakes lasts for 4 years. How many years does a President serve if he or she serves 3 terms?

_____

2. Franklin Delano Rattles was President of the United Snakes for 16 years. How many terms did he serve? _____

3. The election for President of the United Snakes happens every 4 years. The next election will be in 1998. Was there an election in 1990? _____

4. In which years did an election for President of the United Snakes happen during the 1980s? _____

_____

5. Snake representatives serve 2-year terms. Fangella was in Snake Congress from 1984 until 1996. How many terms did she serve? _____

6. Snake Congress has 500 members. More than half of the representatives

must vote for a law to get it passed. At least how many members have to vote for a law to get it passed? _____

7. One law got 12 more votes than half of all the snake representatives. How many votes did the law get? _____

8. Sixty snake representatives did not vote on another law. How many voted? _____

9. To change the Snake Constitution, 100 more than half the representatives must vote to make a change. How many votes are needed to change the Snake Constitution? _____

WRAP IT UP! Hold a pretend election for your favorite animal. How many votes did each of your winners get?

Name: _____

BASEBALL FEVER featuring Woovis the Dog and Judy the Frog

2. In a baseball game, 8 balls were hit. Judy caught 6 of the balls. What fraction did Judy catch? Write your answer in lowest terms. _____

3. After the game, Judy caught $\frac{1}{2}$ of the 12 insect flies that came past. How many flies did she catch? _____

4. Judy caught 5 out of 15 grounders that were hit to her in a baseball game. What fraction of groundballs did she catch? Write your answer in lowest terms. _____

5. Suppose Judy caught 1 more grounder in problem 4. Now what fraction did she catch? Write your answer in lowest terms. _____

6. In the grass, Judy caught 6 out of 18 insects. What fraction of insects did she catch? Write your answer in lowest terms. _____

7. During the baseball game, Judy got a hit 4 out of 10 times at bat. What fraction of the time did Judy get a hit? Write your answer in lowest terms.

_____

8. Woovis got a hit 9 out of 30 times. What fraction of the time did Woovis *not* get a hit? Write your answer in lowest terms. _____

WRAP IT UP! Play baseball, kickball, basketball, or some other game where you have hits and misses. Keep a record of how many hits and misses you make. Express your record as a fraction in lowest terms.

DOCTOR KNOWS BEST featuring Dr. Woovis and Judy the Frog

YOU ANSWER IT!

1. Judy had a full mug of cocoa. She drank $\frac{1}{3}$ of the cocoa in the mug. What fraction of cocoa was left? _____

2. Dr. Woovis drank $\frac{1}{6}$ of a mug of cocoa. After lunch, he drank another $\frac{3}{6}$ of a mug. What fraction of the mug did he drink in all? Write your answer in lowest terms. _____

3. Judy poured $\frac{3}{8}$ of a mug of cocoa into a mug that was $\frac{1}{8}$ full. What fraction of a mug was filled with cocoa? Write your answer in lowest terms. _____

4. Fangella had a full mug of tea. She spilled $\frac{8}{12}$ of the tea. What fraction of tea was left in the mug? Write your answer in lowest terms. _____

5. Fangella added $\frac{6}{12}$ of a mug of tea to what was left in problem 4. In simplest form, what fraction of the mug was full? _____

6. Steve's mug of tea was $\frac{3}{4}$ full. Did Steve's mug have more tea in it than Fangella's mug of tea in problem 5?

_____

7. A glass is $\frac{2}{5}$ full of water. What fraction of a full glass do you need to add to fill the glass completely? _____

8. A glass is $\frac{1}{6}$ full of water. What fraction of a full glass do you need to add to fill the glass halfway? _____

WRAP IT UP! A ladle holds $\frac{3}{8}$ of a cup of water. How many ladles can you add together before you have more than 2 cups of water? What fraction of a cup will you have left over? _____

_____

30

Name: _____

NEW BOOTS featuring Woovis the Dog, and Sal and Al Gator

YOU ANSWER IT!

1. Sal grew 2 inches in March and $1\frac{1}{4}$ inches in April. How many total inches did she grow in these two months? _____

2. Sal grew $1\frac{3}{4}$ inches in May. How much more did she grow in May than in April? Write your answer in lowest terms. _____

3. How many total inches did Sal grow in March, April, and May? _____ _____

4. How many more inches did Sal grow in March than in April? _____

5. Sal grew $\frac{3}{8}$ of an inch in June. How many total inches did she grow in May and June? _____

6. How many more inches did Sal grow in May than in June? _____

7. Al grew $\frac{1}{2}$ of an inch in June. In June, how much more did Al grow than Sal?
_____

8. Over the 3 summer months, Al grew $\frac{1}{2}$ of an inch, $1\frac{2}{3}$ inches, and 2 inches. How many inches did he grow in all?
_____

9. Sal grew 6 inches in 4 months. She grew the same amount each month. How much did she grow each month?
_____

WRAP IT UP! Measure your own growth rate over the year. What was the average number of inches you grew each month?

Name: _____

STUBBED featuring Squirmy Worm and Wendy Spider

YOU ANSWER IT!

1. A cloud poured $\frac{5}{8}$ inches of rain on the ground. The next day it rained $\frac{3}{8}$ of an inch. How many inches did it rain in all? _____

_____

2. In problem 1, how many more inches did it rain on the first day than on the second day? _____

3. Wendy spun a thread of silk $4\frac{1}{2}$ inches long. Then she tied it to a second thread $2\frac{3}{4}$ inches long. What was the total length of the two threads?

_____

4. How much longer was the first thread in problem 3 than the second thread?

_____

5. Squirmy measures $2\frac{1}{8}$ inches in length. Squirmy's Uncle Walter measures 4 inches. How much longer is Uncle Walter than Squirmy? _____

_____

6. Suppose Squirmy grows $\frac{2}{3}$ of an inch this year. How long will he be?

_____

7. Measure this spider thread with a ruler.

_____

Under it, draw a thread that is $3\frac{1}{4}$ inches in length. Which thread is longer? By how much? _____

_____

WRAP IT UP! Write down your height and the heights of your classmates. Then add the numbers together. What is the total height of your class? _____

DANCE FEVER featuring Woovis the Dog and Rowena Pig

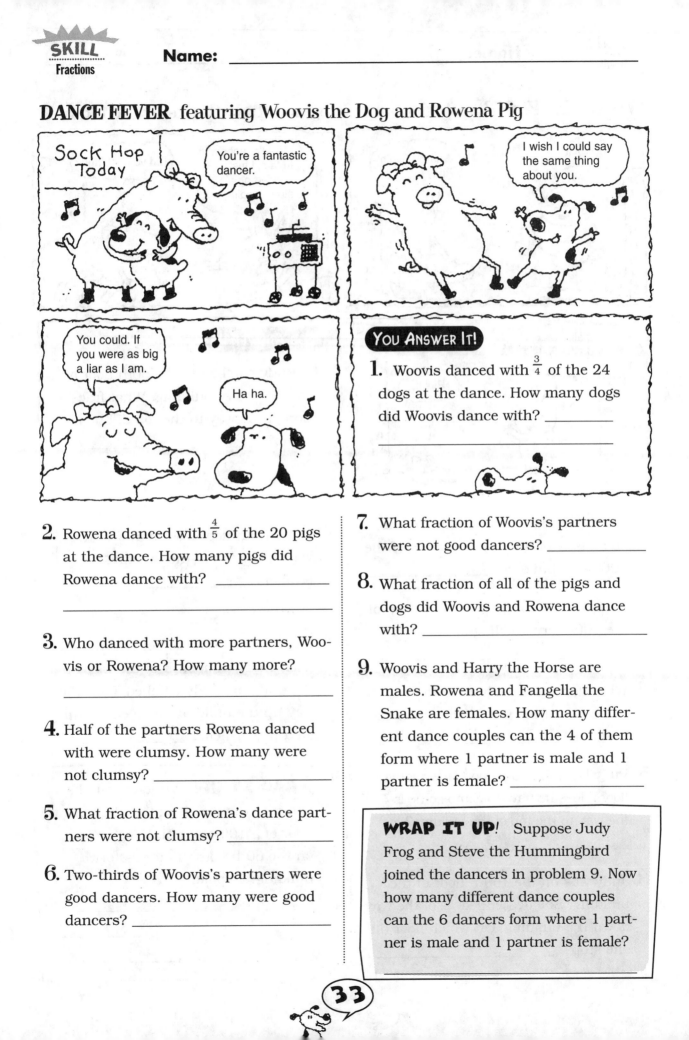

Sock Hop Today

You're a fantastic dancer.

I wish I could say the same thing about you.

You could. If you were as big a liar as I am.

Ha ha.

YOU ANSWER IT!

1. Woovis danced with $\frac{3}{4}$ of the 24 dogs at the dance. How many dogs did Woovis dance with? _____

_____

2. Rowena danced with $\frac{4}{5}$ of the 20 pigs at the dance. How many pigs did Rowena dance with? _____

_____

3. Who danced with more partners, Woovis or Rowena? How many more?

_____

4. Half of the partners Rowena danced with were clumsy. How many were not clumsy? _____

5. What fraction of Rowena's dance partners were not clumsy? _____

6. Two-thirds of Woovis's partners were good dancers. How many were good dancers? _____

7. What fraction of Woovis's partners were not good dancers? _____

8. What fraction of all of the pigs and dogs did Woovis and Rowena dance with? _____

9. Woovis and Harry the Horse are males. Rowena and Fangella the Snake are females. How many different dance couples can the 4 of them form where 1 partner is male and 1 partner is female? _____

WRAP IT UP! Suppose Judy Frog and Steve the Hummingbird joined the dancers in problem 9. Now how many different dance couples can the 6 dancers form where 1 partner is male and 1 partner is female?

_____

Name: _____

WHAT'S HOPPIN'? featuring Judy Frog and Rudy the Red-Nosed Rabbit

YOU ANSWER IT!

1. Rudy climbed to the 50th floor of the 100-story building. What fraction of the way to the top did he climb? _____

2. What floor does Rudy need to climb to so he is $\frac{1}{4}$ of the way to the top of the 100-story building? _____

3. What fraction of the way to the top of the 100-story building is the 20th floor? _____

4. What floor does Rudy need to climb to so he is $\frac{2}{5}$ of the way to the top of the building? _____

5. Rudy is on the 68th floor. How many floors does he have to climb so he is $\frac{3}{4}$ of the way to the top of the building?

_____

6. Judy was on the 100th floor of the building. She descended $\frac{7}{10}$ of the way down the building. On which floor did she stop? _____

7. Is the 30th floor less than $\frac{1}{3}$ of the way to the top of the building? Explain. _____

_____

8. Rudy and Judy were both on the first floor. Rudy climbed $\frac{3}{5}$ of the way up the building. Judy climbed $\frac{3}{4}$ of the way up the building. Who ended up on a higher floor? _____

WRAP IT UP! Which would be closer to the top: Being on the 60th floor of a 100-story building or being on the 60th floor of an 80-story building? Explain.

_____

_____

_____

34

Name: _____

BURNT CAKE featuring Judy Frog and Steve Hummingbird

YOU ANSWER IT!

1. Judy put her cake in the oven at 6:45 p.m. That cake started to burn at 8:30 p.m. How long was the cake in the oven before it began burning? _____

2. Judy's cakes all take the same time to burn. The next day, Judy puts another cake in the over at 12:25 p.m. What time will the cake begin to burn? _____

3. Judy baked an apple pie for $1\frac{1}{3}$ hours. If she started baking the pie at 9:30 a.m., when was it done? _____

4. An apple pie bakes for $1\frac{1}{3}$ hours. When will the pie be done if it is put in the oven at 11:40 a.m.? _____

5. Judy started work at 8:30 a.m. She worked for $8\frac{3}{4}$ hours. What time did she finish work? _____

6. Steve has a job delivering messages. On Monday, he worked from 10:00 a.m. to to 3:10 p.m. How many hours did he work? Write your answer as a mixed number. _____

7. Suppose Steve works the same hours as he did in problem 6 for all 5 days in a week. How many total hours will he work for the week? _____

8. A batch of cookies takes $\frac{3}{4}$ of an hour to bake in the oven. Steve makes 5 batches of cookies one right after the other. How many hours will it take Steve to bake all the cookies?

_____

WRAP IT UP! Find a cookie recipe in a cookbook. How long will it take to make 3 batches of cookies using the cookbook recipe?

LEFTOVERS featuring Woovis the Dog and Fangella the Snake

YOU ANSWER IT!

1. There are 12 snakes in a diner. Five of the snakes order soup. Write a fraction that shows how many snakes order soup. _____
_____

2. Write a fraction that shows how many snakes in the diner did not order soup. _____

3. There are 10 rabbits in the diner. Five of the rabbits order carrot cake. What fraction of the rabbits ordered cake?
_____

4. Nine pigs come into the diner. One third of the pigs order slop. How many pigs order slop? _____

5. Write a fraction that shows how many pigs did not order slop. Write your answer in lowest terms. _____

6. There are 31 animals in the diner. Write a fraction that shows how many of all the animals in the diner are rabbits.
_____

7. Three-quarters of the snakes in the diner and $\frac{2}{5}$ of the rabbits order ice cream. How many snakes and rabbits order ice cream? _____

8. Woovis walks into the diner. How many animals are in the diner now? A total of $\frac{7}{8}$ of all the animals order pie. How many animals order pie? _____

9. What fraction of the animals did *not* order pie? _____

WRAP IT UP! Make a menu that you might see at a place where snakes eat. Then make up a math problem using your menu. Trade papers with a friend and solve each other's problems.

Name: _____

DOCTOR KNOWS BEST AGAIN featuring Dr. Woovis and Rudy the Rabbit

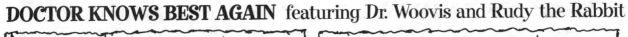

The doctor is [In]

Dr. Woovis, will I be able to play the piano after my broken paw heals?

Of course.

That's great.

Why is that so great?

Because I never knew how to play the piano before.

Woof.

YOU ANSWER IT!

1. After his paw healed, Rudy practiced the piano. The graph below shows his practice record. On which day did he practice the longest? _____

2. On which day or days did Rudy practice less than 5 minutes? _____

3. On which day or days did Rudy practice more than 45 minutes? _____

_____

4. On which day or days did Rudy practice between 10 and 20 minutes?

_____

5. Did Rudy practice more on Day 3 than he did on Day 6? _____

6. Did Rudy practice the same amount of time on Days 4 and 7? _____

7. Was Rudy's combined practice time for Days 6 and 10 more or less than his practice time on on Day 2? _____

8. On Day 15, Rudy practiced for half the time that he practiced on Day 9. How long did he practice on Day 15?

_____

WRAP IT UP! Use Rudy's practice graph to make up more problems to share with a friend.

Name: _____

WHAT'S HOPPIN' AGAIN featuring Judy the Frog and Rudy the Rabbit

YOU ANSWER IT!

1. Look at the graph below. Starting at square X, Judy hopped 4 squares up and 3 squares to the right. In which square did she land? _____

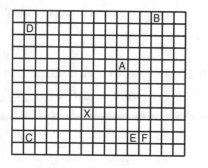

NOTE: Judy and Rudy can hop in vertical and horizontal directions only.

2. Rudy is in square X. Which are the 2 shortest paths he can take to get to square E? _____
_____

3. Judy is in square A. Which are the 2 shortest paths she can take to get to square E? _____
_____

4. Find the 2 shortest paths to get from square X to square D. _____
_____

5. Find 3 paths to get from square D to square E. Does each path contain the same total number of squares? _____
_____
_____

6. Starting at square X, Rudy hopped 6 squares up and 5 squares to the left. How many squares is he from square D? _____

WRAP IT UP! Use the grid to make up some more problems for a friend to try.

Name: _____

NEW JOB featuring Ant Betty and Judy the Frog

2. How many hours did Judy work on Monday? _____

3. How many hours did Judy work on Tuesday? _____

4. How many more hours did Judy work on Tuesday than on Monday? _____

5. On Thursday, Judy worked 7 hours and 15 minutes. Draw what that would look like on the pictograph.

6. On Friday, Judy worked 4 hours and 45 minutes more than she did on Monday. How many hours did Judy work on Friday? Draw your answer in pictograph form.

7. How many hours did Judy work on Monday, Tuesday, and Wednesday? Draw your answer in pictograph form.

8. Did Judy work more hours on Thursday and Friday than she did on Monday, Tuesday, and Wednesday? If so, how many more hours? _____

_____

WRAP IT UP! How many hours do you spend in school a week? Make a pictograph of your answer.

Name: _____

SPECIAL DELIVERY featuring Ant Betty and Fangella the Snake

YOU ANSWER IT!

1. One gallon contains 4 quarts. How many quarts are there in 2 gallons of milk? _____

_____

2. How many quarts are there in 7 gallons of milk? _____

3. Fangella had 20 quarts of milk. How many gallons does that equal? _____

_____

4. Fangella poured 10 quarts of milk into gallon containers. How many gallon containers did she fill? How many quarts were left over? _____

_____

5. There are 12 inches in 1 foot. How many inches long is a 4-foot snake?

_____

6. A group of ants formed a line 96 inches long. How long was the line in feet?

_____

7. The ants were carrying a string of foot-long hot dogs that was 54 inches long. How many whole feet was this? How many inches were left over?

_____

8. There are 2 pints in 1 quart. How many pints are in 1 gallon?

_____

How many pints are in 3 gallons?

_____

WRAP IT UP! Use a yardstick to measure yourself in inches, feet, and yards. Which unit of measure seems to work best for measuring height? Explain your answer.

Name: _____

MONEY BACK featuring Woovis the Dog and Sal and Al Gator

YOU ANSWER IT!

1. Sal and Al plant their bird seeds in a square garden that measures 6 feet on each of its 4 sides. What is the perimeter of their garden?

_____

2. What is the area of Sal and Al's bird seed garden in square feet? _____
_____

3. Al's flower garden is a rectangle that is 8 yards long and 3 yards wide. What is the garden's perimeter? _____
_____

4. One yard equals 3 feet. What is the perimeter of Al's garden in feet?

_____

5. What is the area of Al's garden in square yards? _____

6. What is the length and width of Al's garden in feet? _____

7. What is the area of Al's garden in square feet? _____

8. Woovis has his own garden that is shaped like a rectangle. It has a width of 5 yards and an area of 55 square yards. What is the garden's length?

_____

9. What is the perimeter of Woovis's garden in feet? _____

WRAP IT UP! Compare a 6 foot by 2 foot rectangle with a 4 foot by 3 foot rectangle. How do their areas compare? How do their perimeters compare? Explain. _____
_____
_____

Name: _____

FUN BOX featuring Ant Betty and Fangella the Snake

YOU ANSWER IT!

1. Each square side of the box is 8 inches long. What is the perimeter of 1 square side? _____

2. Each square side of another box is 18 inches long. What is the perimeter of one square side? _____

3. Each side of a square is 3.25 inches long. What is the square's perimeter?

_____

4. The length of a rectangle is 12 feet. The width of the rectangle is 8 feet. What is the rectangle's perimeter?

_____

5. Another rectangle has a length of 8.25 inches and a width of 5.5 inches. What is the rectangle's perimeter?

_____

6. A square has a perimeter of 44 feet. What is the length of each of the square's sides? _____

7. A pentagon has 5 sides that each are 2.4 inches long. What is the pentagon's perimeter? _____

8. A pentagon's perimeter is 62 inches. It's 5 sides are all the same length. What is the length of each side?

_____

9. A hexagon has 6 sides that each measure 2.4 inches. What is the hexagon's perimeter? _____

WRAP IT UP! Use a ruler or a tape measure to measure the perimeter of different objects in your classroom.

Name: _____

PIE AND PI featuring Woovis the Dog and Moovis the Cow

THE MOOVIS AND WOOVIS SHOW

I'm Woovis.

I'm Moovis.

Hey Woovis, which is the **left** side of this blueberry pie?

That's easy. It's the part you haven't eaten yet.

YOU ANSWER IT!

1. The pie pan has a radius (center to outside edge distance) of 6 inches. Radius = r. Use the formula C = 2 x π x r to find the C, the circumference or distance around the outside of the pan. The number π equals 3.14. _____

2. What is the circumference around a pie with a radius of 12 inches? _____

3. The diameter, or distance all the way across a circle is 4 feet. What is the circumference of the circle? _____

4. Use the formula A = πr² to find the area of a pie with a 6-inch radius in square inches. _____

5. What is the area of a pie with a 3.5 meter radius? _____

6. Which is larger — the circumference of a circle with a 50-foot diameter or the circumference of a circle with a 25-foot radius? Explain. _____
_____

7. A figure-8 is made of two circles with 4-inch diameters. What is the total area of the space inside both circles? _____
_____

d = 4 in

d = 4 in

8. What is the circumference of the circle below? _____

d = 20 in

9. What is the distance around the outside of the shaded half of the circle? What is the area of the shaded half of the circle?
_____

WRAP IT UP! Draw a circle. Measure its diameter. Measure its circumference using a piece of string. The circumference is about how many times the length of the diameter? _____

SNOOZER featuring Woovis the Dog and Moovis the Cow

YOU ANSWER IT!

1. Moovis snores 720 times in 1 hour. How many times does she snore in half an hour? _____

2. There are 60 minutes in 1 hour. How many times does Moovis snore in 15 minutes? _____

3. How many times does Moovis snore in 1 minute? _____

4. Harry the Horse snores 660 times in 1 hour. How many times does he snore in 1 minute? _____

5. In 2 hours, how many more times will Moovis snore than Harry? _____

6. Steve the Hummingbird snores 84 times in 6 minutes. How many times does he snore in 1 hour? _____

7. Steve snores twice as fast as Woovis. How many times does Woovis snore in 1 hour? _____

8. Judy snores 132 times in 12 minutes. Does she snore faster than Steve? _____

9. Ant Betty snores 1.5 times faster than Steve. How many times does Ant Betty snore in 1 hour? _____

WRAP IT UP! How many time does Ant Betty snore in 20 minutes? How many times does she snore in 3 minutes? _____

Name: _____

PULSATIONS featuring Dr. Woovis and Rudy the Red-Nosed Rabbit

YOU ANSWER IT!

1. Rudy's heart beats 80 times in 1 minute. How many times will it beat in 3 minutes? _____

2. How many times will Rudy's heart beat in 10 minutes? _____

3. How many times will Rudy's heart beat in 30 minutes? _____

4. There are 60 minutes in 1 hour. How many times will Rudy's heart beat in 1 hour? _____

5. Woovis measures Harry the Horse's heart beat. In 30 seconds, Harry's heart beats 38 times. How many times will his heart beat in 1 minute?

_____

6. Does Harry's heat beat faster or slower than Rudy's heart? By how much does Harry's heart beat faster or slower?

_____

7. There are 60 seconds in 1 minute. Judy the Frog's heart beats 20 times in 15 seconds. How many times does her heart beat in 1 minute? _____

8. How many times will Judy's heart beat in half an hour? _____

9. Woovis's heart beats 5,400 times in 1 hour. How many times does it beat in 1 day? How many times does it beat in 3 days? _____

Math is lots and lots of fun!

WRAP IT UP! How many times does Woovis's heart beat in 1 week?

_____

Name: _____

HUMS featuring Harry the Horse and Steve the Hummingbird

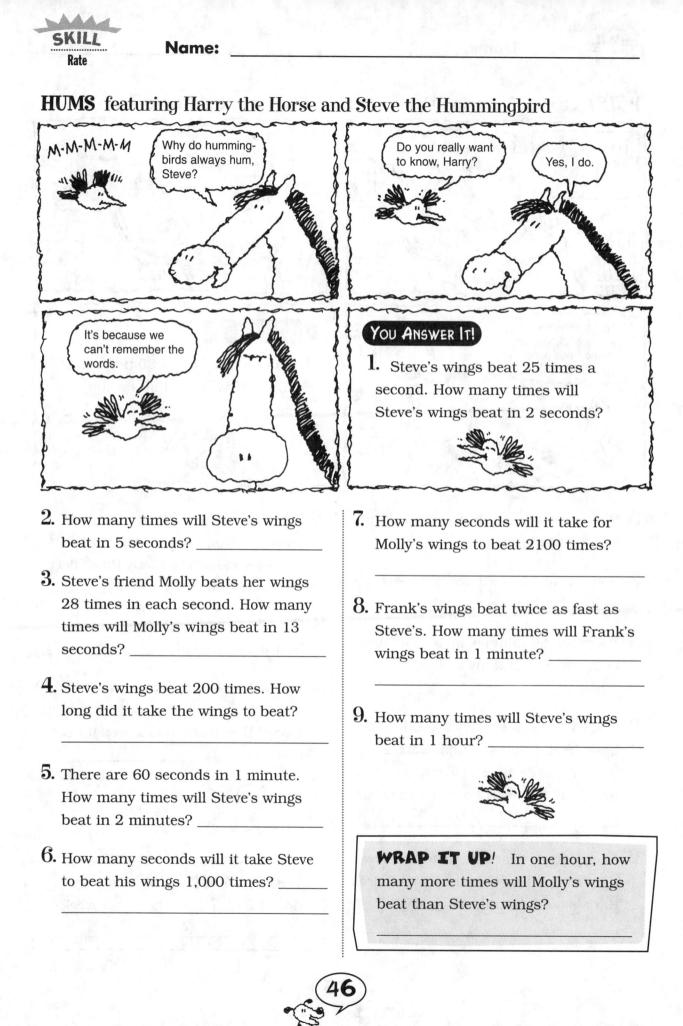

M·M·M·M·M

Why do humming-birds always hum, Steve?

Do you really want to know, Harry?

Yes, I do.

It's because we can't remember the words.

YOU ANSWER IT!

1. Steve's wings beat 25 times a second. How many times will Steve's wings beat in 2 seconds?

2. How many times will Steve's wings beat in 5 seconds? _____

3. Steve's friend Molly beats her wings 28 times in each second. How many times will Molly's wings beat in 13 seconds? _____

4. Steve's wings beat 200 times. How long did it take the wings to beat?

_____

5. There are 60 seconds in 1 minute. How many times will Steve's wings beat in 2 minutes? _____

6. How many seconds will it take Steve to beat his wings 1,000 times? _____

_____

7. How many seconds will it take for Molly's wings to beat 2100 times?

_____

8. Frank's wings beat twice as fast as Steve's. How many times will Frank's wings beat in 1 minute? _____

_____

9. How many times will Steve's wings beat in 1 hour? _____

WRAP IT UP! In one hour, how many more times will Molly's wings beat than Steve's wings?

_____

46

Name: _____

SPEED TRAP featuring Officer Woovis and Rowena Pig

YOU ANSWER IT!

1. A car traveled 36 miles per hour (mph) in a 15 mph speed zone. How much over the speed limit was the car traveling? _____

2. Rowena was driving a car 21 miles over the 25 mph speed limit. How fast was she going? _____

3. Yesterday, Rowena went 29 mph in a 40 mph speed zone. How far under the speed limit was she traveling?

_____

4. Harry the Horse's car traveled 35 miles in each hour. How many miles did Harry drive his car in 5 hours?

_____

5. Rowena's car traveled 17 miles in each hour. How many miles did she drive her car in 12 hours? _____

6. Rudy the Red Nosed Rabbit drove his car for 4 hours and covered 200 miles. The car traveled the same num-ber of miles in each hour. How many miles did the car travel each hour?

_____

7. Rowena drove her car 3 times. The first trip was 7 miles, the second trip was 22 miles, and the third trip was 13 miles. What was the average driving distance for the 3 trips? _____

8. Rowena drove her car 4 more times. The total miles covered in those 4 trips was 42 miles. What was the average driving distance for Rowena's 7 total trips? _____

WRAP IT UP! Use a road map to plan a trip that is about 100 miles from your home that includes 4 stops. What is the average distance between stops on your trips?

47

Name: _____

FAMILY REUNION PICNIC featuring Woovis the Dog and Rowena Pig

YOU ANSWER IT!

1. What was the ratio of grandparents to uncles at the picnic? Write your answer in lowest terms.

   _____

Write all ratios in lowest terms.

2. What was the ratio of uncles to cousins at the picnic? _____
   _____

3. Eight of the cousins at the picnic were boys. How many of the cousins were girls? What was the ratio of girl cousins to boy cousins? _____
   _____

4. What was the ratio of boy cousins to all cousins at the picnic? _____

5. What was the ratio of girl cousins to uncles at the picnic? _____

6. What was the ratio of grandparents to cousins and uncles? _____
   _____

7. What was the ratio of ants to all others at the picnic? _____

8. Ten percent or 10 out of every 100 ants were red. How many of the ants at the picnic were red? _____

9. Four hundred of the 800 ants were late to the picnic. What percent of the ants were late? _____

So long! Hope you had fun!

WRAP IT UP! Seventy percent or 70 out of every 100 ants at the picnic were hungry. How many of the ants were not hungry?

_____

ANSWERS

YOU DON'T SAY: page 9

1. They told 11 jokes in all.
2. The audience laughed at 9 jokes.
3. Five jokes were not udderly ridiculous.
4. They were on stage for 24 minutes after the intermission.
5. Woovis told 8 jokes after intermission.
6. The show played for 15 nights in all.
7. Woovis earned $6 for each show. Moovis earned $4 for each show.

Wrap It Up! Answers will vary.

LATE TO WORK: page 10

1. Judy slept for 10 hours in all.
2. That is 9 1/2 hours of sleep.
3. She should wake up at 8 a.m.
4. Al Gator slept for 9 hours.
5. He slept for 11 hours.
6. Judy worked 3 1/2 hours after her break.
7. Al actually worked 3 hours.
8. The actual time is 7:30 p.m.

Wrap It Up! Judy should set her alarm for 7:30 a.m.

ROUND TRIP: page 11

1. The trip is 8 miles long.
2. The trip is 12 miles long.
3. The trip is 20 miles long.
4. The shortest trip is from the Old Travel Agency, to the Old Tree, to the Old Pond. This trip is 8 miles long.
5. Woovis started at the Old Travel Agency and went to the Old Tree, the Old Mill, and back to the Travel Agency.
6. The trip from the Old Travel Agency to the Old Mill, Old Tree, and Old Pond covers 9 miles.
7. The trip from the Old Travel Agency to the Old Tree, to the Old Mill, to the Old Pond.

Wrap It Up! Answers will vary.

THE TEXAN: page 12

1. There are 345 miles between El Paso and Lubbock.
2. Squirmy traveled 664 miles in all.
3. Rowena traveled 75 fewer miles.
4. A round-trip would cover 708 miles.
5. The route from Dallas to Austin, to San Antonio, to Brownsville.
6. The route from San Antonio to Houston, to Dallas, to Fort Worth, to Lubbock.
7. The shortest route is from San Antonio to Austin, to Dallas, to Fort Worth, to Lubbock. The route covers 617 miles.

Wrap It Up! Answers will vary.

DOGGY DINER: page 13

1. Two Trough Dinners would cost $9.90.
2. A Trough Dinner and an order of Regular Slop would cost $8.90.
3. A cup of Mush, one order of Scraps, and one order of Swill would cost $4.74.
4. Fifteen dollars is enough money. You know because $4.95 is less than $5.00. 3 times $4.95 must be less than 3 times $5, or $15.
5. Yes. She will get back $1.76 in change.
6. Four orders of Deluxe Slop cost 5 cents more.
7. Rowena also ordered Scraps.
8. Purvis needs $2.85 more.
9. She would need $42.16.

Wrap It Up! Answers will vary.

PHONEY BALONEY: page 14

1. Six thousand, seven hundred, eighty-nine
2. The digit 8 occupies the tens' place.
3. The digit 9 is in the ones' place.
4. 6,790; 7,000
5. Four hundred, seventy-six thousand, seven hundred, eighty-nine
6. The digit 4 is in the hundred thousands' place.
7. The digit 7 occupies the ten thousands' place and the hundreds' place.

8. The digit 2 occupies the millions' place.

9. The digit 3 is in the tens' place. The digit 4 is in the tenths' place.

Wrap It Up! Answers will vary. In a 10 digit number, the first three digits are in the billions' place, 100 millions' place, and 10 millions' place.

TAXI, TAXI!: page 15

1. The movie will end at 12:45 p.m.

2. The second show begins at 1 p.m.

3. The third show began at 2:45 p.m. No, he will not arrive on time.

4. Yes. He can go to the 6:15 p.m. show that ends at 7:45 p.m.

5. Twice. The movie is shown at the beginning of the hour at 1 p.m. and 8 p.m.

6. The movie will be shown at 4 p.m.

7. Yes. Both movies are shown at 6:15 p.m.

Wrap It Up! Answers will vary. Show times are often staggered to control the flow of people traffic.

RABBIT FEET: page 16

1. Four rabbits have 16 feet.

2. There are 6 rabbits in the group.

3. Twenty legs were doing cartwheels.

4. They bought 132 sneakers.

5. They bought 66 pairs of sneakers.

6. There were 9 animals.

7. Fifty legs are walking in all.

8. There are 182 legs in all.

Wrap It Up! Answers will vary.

SEVEN-KERPLUNK!: page 17

1. He takes 40 steps.

2. She takes 9 steps with each of her 8 legs.

3. Susan takes 40 more steps than Sharon.

4. He takes 240 steps in all.

5. She takes 49 steps with her other legs.

6. She takes 136 steps in all.

7. She took 3 more steps.

8. No. Gary takes 156 steps. The spiders took 224 steps.

Wrap It Up! Answers will vary.

STAIRWAY TO THE TOP: page 18

1. She climbed 18 steps.

2. She climbed 45 steps.

3. He ended up on the 5th floor.

4. He walked up 54 steps.

5. He descended 72 steps.

6. She ended up on the 5th floor.

7. They both ended up on the 5th floor.

8. She had to walk up 36 steps.
   (3 floors x 12 = 36 steps).

Wrap It Up! The new answer would be 35 steps.

GO SKATING: page 19

1. It will cost 70 cents to rent 2 pairs of skates.

2. It will cost $3.45 to rent skates and skate.

3. The total cost will be $6.90.

4. The cost will be $4.15.

5. It will cost $5.85 for the two of them to go skating.

6. It will cost $8.30 to rent skates and go skating.

7. The four spent $12.40 to skate.

8. The animal has 6 legs.

Wrap It Up! It will cost $55.20 to rent skates and skate. They would save $11.20 if they brought their own skates.

MOUSE TRAP: page 20

1. Three regular mousetraps will cost $14.85.

2. Twelve regular mousetraps will cost $59.40.

3. Five deluxe mousetraps will cost $32.45.

4. Five deluxe mousetraps cost $2.75 more than 6 regular mousetraps.

5. The mousetraps will cost $78.54.

6. Harry can save $18.85.

7. She can buy 34 mousetraps (1 case of 24 plus 10 individual traps at $4.95 each.)

8. A case of deluxe mousetraps costs $125.

9. A customer can buy 27 deluxe mousetraps with $150.

Wrap It Up! Answers will vary.

CAMOUFLAGE: page 21

1. Eight cows were in each tree.
2. There were 32 animals in each tree.
3. There were 6 trees in all.
4. There were 35 cows in all.
5. Six cows hid in each tree.
6. The cow gave 72 buckets of milk.
7. They spent 8 weeks on the road.
8. There were 21 cows in each group.
9. Sixteen cows jumped over the fence each minute.

Wrap It Up! Answers will vary.

NON-TOXIC: page 22

1. Fangella will stick her tongue out 15 times in 1 minute.
2. Fangella will stick her tongue out 45 times in 3 minutes.
3. Fangella will stick her tongue out 450 times in half an hour.
4. Fangella is 12 times longer than Squirmy.
5. She traveled 15 miles each day.
6. There were 43 snakes in each group.
7. Fangella collected $516.
8. There were 42 snakes in the group.

Wrap It Up! Answers will vary.

CARROT SOUP: page 23

1. He could make 4 pots of soup with 2 carrots left over.
2. He needs 168 carrots to make the soup. He needs 112 carrots to make the soup.
3. He can make 9 pots of soup. He can make 18 pots of soup.
4. He can make 14 pots of soup with 2 carrots left over.
5. He can make 9 pots of 7-carrot soup. He can make 4 pots of 14-carrot soup. The 14-carrot soup will have 7 carrrots left over.
6. He had 73 carrots when he started.
7. He can make 20 pots of soup.
8. He can make 200 pots of soup.

Wrap It Up! Rudy can make twice as many pots of 7-carrot soup as 14-carrot soup no matter how many carrots he begins with.

GOLF PRO: page 24

1. Each player will win $12,500.
2. Each player will win $6,250.
3. There would be 20 players.
4. The winner won $50,000. The other two players each won $25,000.
5. The winner won $52,000.
6. The 4th-place finisher won $4,000.
7. They each won $3,000.

Wrap It Up! Answers will vary. Check to see that each successive finisher receives twice as much prize money as the next lowest finisher.

NIGHT SCHOOL: page 25

1. It will take her about 5 hours to finish the book.
2. It will take him about 7 hours to finish the book.
3. He can read about 348 pages in 6 hours.
4. It will take about 9 hours for Woovis to read the book.
5. It will take Moovis about 10 to 11 hours to read the book.
6. She can buy *Moo Over Miami* and *The Big Moo* for under $5. She can buy *Moo Over Miami*, and *Cow for a Day* for under $6. She can buy *Cow for a Day*, and *The Moo Lagoon* for under $10.
7. Woovis needs about $15 to buy all 4 books.

Wrap It Up! Answers will vary.

THE BIG DEAL: page 26

1. They would cost $300.00.
2. The cost of the stickers and notebook was closer to $5.00
3. The cost of 1 movie ticket rounded to the nearest dollar was $6.00.
4. Woovis's change rounded to the nearest dollar was $4.00.
5. The cost of the popcorn rounded to the nearest dollar was $3.00.
6. The cost of the popcorn rounded to the nearest 10 cents was $3.20.

51

7. The total amount of money spent rounded to the nearest dollar is $12.00.

8. The total cost of the 3 items rounded to the nearest dollar is $98.00.

9. No. Wendy's change is $1.87.

Wrap It Up! Answers will vary.

THE DAY OF THE DENTIST: page 27

1. Tiger has 21 teeth now.

2. Tiger Smith has 35 stripes.

3. Yes. Tiger Brown has 32 stripes.

4. She saw 6 patients yesterday.

5. There are 4 spiders in the group.

6. The spiders. They have 32 legs and the tigers have 28 legs.

7. There are 64 animal legs standing now.

Wrap It Up! Tiger Jones played for 16 hours on Sunday and for 4 hours on Friday. He played 12 hours longer on Sunday than he did on Friday.

POLITICS: page 28

1. The President serves 12 years.

2. He served 4 terms.

3. There was an election in 1990.

4. The election happened in 1982 and 1986.

5. She served 6 terms.

6. A total of 251 members have to vote to pass a law.

7. The law got 262 votes.

8. A total of 440 representatives voted.

9. 350 must vote to make change.

Wrap It Up! Answers will vary.

BASEBALL FEVER: page 29

1. $\frac{1}{2}$

2. $\frac{3}{4}$ of the baseballs were caught.

3. Judy caught 6 flies.

4. Judy caught $\frac{1}{3}$ of the groundballs.

5. She caught $\frac{2}{5}$ of the groundballs.

6. Judy caught $\frac{1}{3}$ of the insects.

7. Judy got a hit $\frac{2}{5}$ of the time.

8. Woovis did not get a hit $\frac{7}{10}$ of the time.

Wrap It Up! Answers will vary.

DOCTOR KNOWS BEST: page 30

1. $\frac{2}{3}$ of the cocoa was left.

2. He drank $\frac{2}{3}$ of the mug.

3. $\frac{1}{2}$ of the mug was filled with cocoa.

4. $\frac{1}{3}$ of the tea was left in the mug.

5. $\frac{5}{6}$ of the mug was full.

6. No. $\frac{3}{4}$ is smaller than $\frac{5}{6}$

7. You need to add $\frac{3}{5}$ of a full glass.

8. You need to add $\frac{1}{3}$ of a full glass.

Wrap It Up! You can add 6 ladles. $\frac{1}{4}$ of a cup will be left over.

NEW BOOTS: page 31

1. Sal grew $3\frac{1}{4}$ inches in the 2 months.

2. Sal grew $\frac{1}{2}$ inch more.

3. Sal grew a total of 5 inches.

4. Sal grew $\frac{3}{4}$ inch.

5. Sal grew a total of $2\frac{1}{8}$ inches.

6. Sal grew $1\frac{3}{8}$ inches more.

7. Al grew $\frac{1}{8}$ inch more than Sal.

8. Al grew $4\frac{1}{6}$ inches in all.

9. Sal grew $1\frac{1}{2}$ inches each month.

Wrap It Up! Answers will vary.

STUBBED: page 32

1. It rained I inch.

2. It rained $\frac{1}{4}$ inch more on the first day than on the second day.

3. The two threads are $7\frac{1}{4}$ inches long.

4. The first thread was $1\frac{3}{4}$ inches longer.

5. Uncle Walter is $1\frac{7}{8}$ inches longer than Squirmy.

6. Squirmy will be $2\frac{19}{24}$ inches long.

7. The $3\frac{1}{4}$-inch thread is 1 inch longer than the first ($2\frac{1}{4}$-inch) thread.

Wrap It Up! Answers will vary.

DANCE FEVER: page 33

1. Woovis danced with 18 dogs.
2. Rowena danced with 16 pigs.
3. Woovis danced with 2 more partners.
4. Eight partners were not clumsy.
5. $\frac{1}{2}$ of Rowena's partners were not clumsy.
6. Twelve of Woovis's partners were good dancers.
7. $\frac{1}{3}$ of Woovis's partners were not good dancers.
8. Woovis and Rowena danced with $\frac{17}{22}$ of the dance partners.
9. Four different couples can be formed: Woovis and Rowena; Woovis and Fangella; Harry and Rowena; Harry and Fangella.

Wrap It Up! Nine different couples can be formed: Steve and Judy; Steve and Rowena; Steve and Fangella; Woovis and Judy; Woovis and Rowena; Woovis and Fangella; Harry and Judy; Harry and Rowena; Harry and Fangella.

WHAT'S HOPPIN'?: page 34

1. Rudy climbed $\frac{1}{2}$ of the way to the top.
2. Rudy needs to climb to the 25th floor.
3. The 20th floor is $\frac{1}{5}$ of the way to the top.
4. Rudy needs to climb to the 40th floor.
5. Rudy needs to climb 7 floors.
6. Judy stopped on the 30th floor.
7. The 30th floor is less than $\frac{1}{3}$ of the way up the building. $\frac{1}{3}$ of the way up the building is approximately the 33rd floor.
8. Judy ended up on a higher floor.

Wrap It Up! Being on the 60th floor of an 80-story building would be higher. Being on the 60th floor of an 80-story is $\frac{3}{4}$ the way up the building. Being on the 60th floor of an 100-story building is $\frac{3}{5}$ the way up the building. $\frac{3}{4}$ is greater than $\frac{3}{5}$.

BURNT CAKE: page 35

1. The cake was in the oven for 1 hour and 45 minutes before it began burning.
2. The cake will begin burning at 2:10 p.m.
3. The pie was done at 10:50 a.m.
4. The pie will be done at 1:00 p.m.
5. She finished work at 5:15 p.m.
6. Steve worked $5\frac{1}{6}$ hours.
7. Steve worked $25\frac{5}{6}$ hours.
8. It will take $3\frac{3}{4}$ hours to bake all the cookies.

Wrap It Up! Answers will vary.

LEFTOVERS: page 36

1. $\frac{5}{12}$ of the snakes order soup.
2. $\frac{7}{12}$ of the snakes did not order soup.
3. $\frac{1}{2}$ of the rabbits ordered cake.
4. Three pigs order slop.
5. $\frac{2}{3}$ of the pigs did not order slop.
6. $\frac{10}{31}$ of the animals are rabbits.
7. Thirteen snakes and rabbits order ice cream.
8. Thirty-two animals are in the diner. Twenty-eight animals order pie.
9. $\frac{1}{8}$ of the animals did not order pie.

Wrap It Up! Answers will vary.

DOCTOR KNOWS BEST AGAIN: page 37

1. Rudy practiced the longest on Day 8.
2. Rudy practiced less than 5 minutes on Day 5.
3. Rudy practiced more than 45 minutes on Days 8, 9, and 11.
4. Rudy practiced between 10 and 20 minutes on Day 10.
5. Yes.
6. Yes.
7. Less.
8. 25 minutes.

Wrap It Up! Answers will vary.

WHAT'S HOPPIN' AGAIN: page 38

1. Judy landed in square A.
2. Down 2 squares and 4 squares to the right.

Four squares to the right and down 2 squares.

3. One square to the right and 6 squares down. Six squares down and 1 square to the right.

4. Seven squares up and 5 squares to the left. Five squares to the left and 7 squares up.

5. Answers will vary. Each path does not have to have the same number of squares.

6. He is 1 squares down from square D.

Wrap It Up! Answers will vary.

NEW JOB: page 39

1. Each circle stands for 1 hour.

2. Judy worked for 3 hours and 15 minutes.

3. Yes. Judy worked $5\frac{1}{2}$ hours on Tuesday.

4. Judy worked for 2 hours and 15 minutes more.

5. ●●●●●●◖

6. She worked for 8 hours:

●●●●●●●●

7. Judy worked $13\frac{1}{2}$ hours:

●●●●●●●●●●●●●◖

8. Yes, she worked 1 hour and 45 minutes more.

Wrap It Up! Answers will vary.

SPECIAL DELIVERY: page 40

1. There are 8 quarts in 2 gallons of milk.

2. There are 28 quarts in 7 gallons of milk.

3. Twenty quarts of milk equals 5 gallons.

4. She filled 2 gallons and there were 2 quarts left over.

5. The snake is 48 inches long.

6. The line was 8 feet long.

7. The string of hot dogs was 4 whole feet with 6 inches left over.

8. There are 8 pints in 1 gallon. There are 24 pints in 3 gallons.

Wrap It Up! Answers will vary. The conventional units used to measure height are feet and inches.

MONEY BACK: page 41

1. The perimeter is 24 feet.

2. The area is 36 square feet.

3. The perimeter is 22 yards.

4. The perimeter is 66 feet.

5. The area is 24 square yards.

6. The length is 24 feet. The width is 9 feet.

7. The area is 216 square feet.

8. The length is 11 yards.

9. The perimeter is 96 feet.

Wrap It Up! Answers will vary.

FUN BOX: page 42

1. The perimeter is 32 inches.

2. The perimeter is 72 inches.

3. The perimeter is 13 inches.

4. The perimeter is 40 feet.

5. The perimeter is 27.5 inches.

6. Each side is 11 feet long.

7. The perimeter is 12 inches.

8. Each side is 12.4 inches long.

9. The perimeter is 14.4 inches long.

Wrap It Up! Answers will vary.

PIE AND PI: page 43

1. The circumference is 37.68 inches.

2. The circumference is 75.36 inches.

3. The circumference is 12.56 feet.

4. The area is 113.04 square inches.

5. The area is 38.47 square meters.

6. They are the same. A circle with a 50-foot diameter has a 25-foot radius.

7. The total area is 25.12 square inches.

8. The circumference is 62.80 inches.

9. The distance is 31.40 inches. The area is 157 square inches.

Wrap It Up! About 3 times as large. This makes sense when you look at the formula.: $C = 2\pi r$ or $C = \pi d$. This means that the circumference is 3.14 (about 3) times the length of the diameter.

SNOOZER: page 44

1. Moovis snores 360 times in half an hour.

2. Moovis snores 180 times in 15 minutes.

3. Moovis snores 12 times in 1 minute.

4. Harry snores 11 times in 1 minute.

5. Moovis will snore 120 more times.

6. Steve snores 840 times in 1 hour.

7. Woovis snores 420 times in 1 hour.

8. No. Steve snores 168 times in 12 minutes.

9. Ant Betty snores 1,260 times in 1 hour.

Wrap It Up! Ant Betty snores 420 times in 20 minutes. She snores 63 times in 3 minutes.

PULSATIONS: page 45

1. Rudy's heart will beat 240 times in 3 minutes.

2. Rudy's heart will beat 800 times in 10 minutes.

3. Rudy's heart will beat 2,400 times in 30 minutes.

4. Rudy's heart will beat 4,800 times in 1 hour.

5. Harry's heart will beat 76 times in 1 minute.

6. Harry's heart beats slower by 4 beats per minute.

7. Judy's heart beats 80 times in 1 minute.

8. Judy's heart beats 2,400 times in half an hour.

9. Woovis's heart beats 129,600 times in 1 day. It beats 388,800 times in 3 days.

Wrap It Up! Woovis's heart beats 907,200 times in 1 week.

HUMS: page 46

1. Steve's wings beat 50 times in 2 seconds.

2. Steve's wings will beat 125 times.

3. Molly's wings will beat 364 times.

4. It took 8 seconds.

5. Steve's wings will beat 3,000 times.

6. It will take 40 seconds.

7. It will take 75 seconds.

8. Frank's wings will beat 3,000 times.

9. Steve's wings will beat 90,000 times.

Wrap It Up! Molly's wings will beat 10,800 more times.

SPEED TRAP: page 47

1. He was driving 21 miles over the speed limit.

2. Rowena was going 46 miles per hour.

3. Rowena was traveling 11 miles under the speed limit.

4. He drove 175 miles.

5. She drove 204 miles.

6. The car covered 50 miles each hour.

7. The average mileage was 14 miles.

8. The average mileage was 12 miles.

Wrap It Up! Answers will vary.

FAMILY REUNION PICNIC: page 48

1. The ratio was 1:3.

2. The ratio was 1:2.

3. Sixteen cousins were girls. The ratio was 2:1.

4. The ratio was 1:3.

5. The ratio was 4:3.

6. The ratio was 1:9.

7. The ratio was 20:1.

8. Eighty ants were red.

9. Fifty percent of the ants were late.

Wrap It Up! A total of 240 ants were not hungry.

NOTES